Can you find...
1001 Pirate Things?

igloobooks

Can you find 1001 Pirate Things?

Ahoy me hearties! Welcome to a pirate adventure! There's all sorts of things going on at Pirate Island, from big parties to exciting treasure hunts. Each picture in this book has lots of different and interesting things for you to search and find. In fact, there are over 1000 things to find on Pirate Island! Swashbuckling Sid and One-eyed Eddie are in each picture, so you need to find them first. Then each page has little pictures to show you what else you need to search for, from gold doubloons to scurrying rats!

Swashbuckling Sid

One-eyed Eddie

Let's have a practice. Can you spot Swashbuckling Sid and One-eyed Eddie in the picture on the opposite page. Once you've found them, see if you can spot these items as well:

2 Canons

5 Eye Patches

10 Mice

Yo! Ho! Ho!

There's lots going on aboard the Mighty Barnacle today! Can you spot Swashbuckling Sid and One-eyed Eddie amongst all of the other pirates?

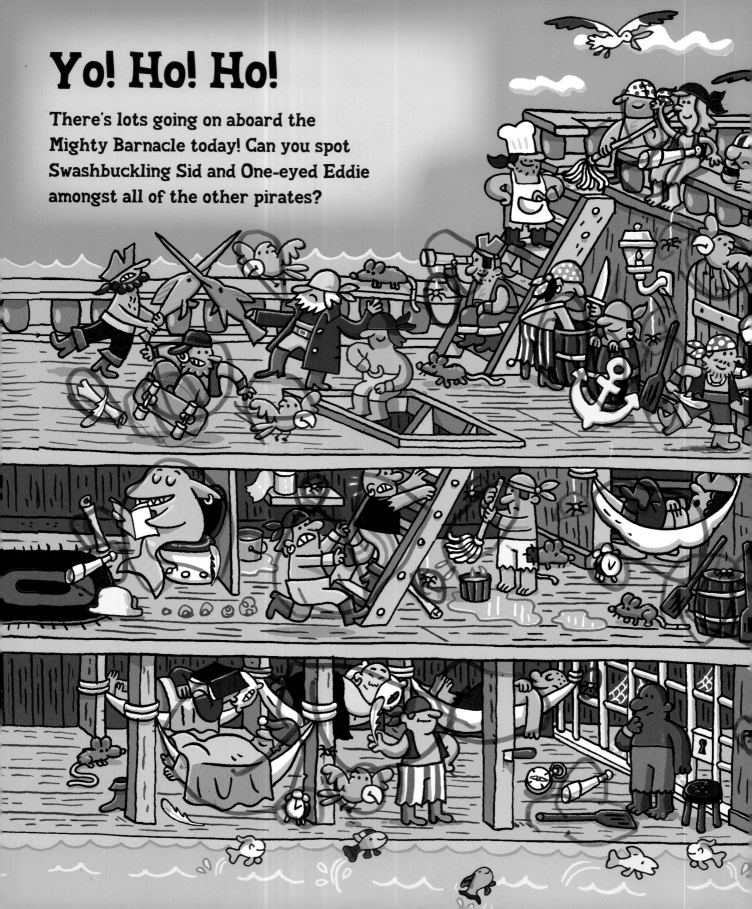

Once you've found Sid and Eddie, see if you can find these things, too.

1 Skateboard

2 Clocks

3 Mops

4 Oars

5 Barrels

6 Hammocks

7 Pieces of Parchment

8 Parrots

9 Telescopes

10 Gold Earrings

20 Spiders

Davey Jones' Locker

In the depth of the deep, blue sea, the pirates have found an ancient shipwreck! Can you spot Swashbuckling Sid and One-eyed Eddie swimming around?

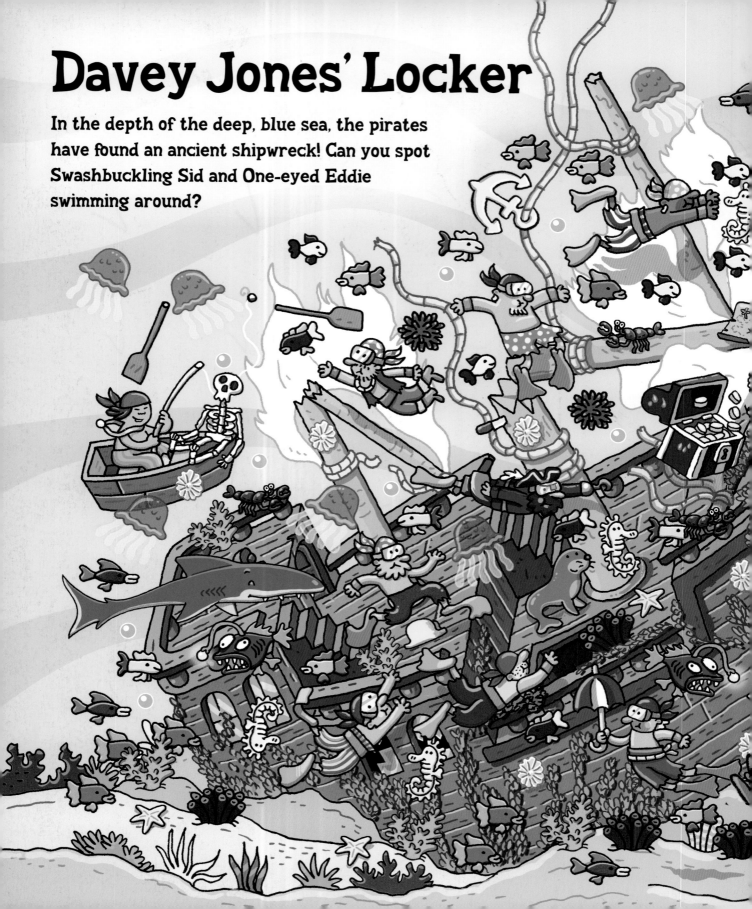

See if you can find these things on the treasure map, too.

1 Treasure Chest

2 Camels

3 Vultures

8 Bones

9 Shark Fins

10 Footprints

20 Flies

Pieces Of Eight!

The pirates have found lots of treasure in a hidden cave!
Can you spot Swashbuckling Sid and One-eyed Eddie
amongst all of the treasure chests?

4 Seagulls

5 Gold Statues

6 Pearl Necklaces

7 Starfish

Can spot these things hidden in the cave, as well.

1 Boat

2 Torches

3 Skull and Crossbones

8 Crowns

9 Silver Goblets

10 Bats

20 Gold Doubloons

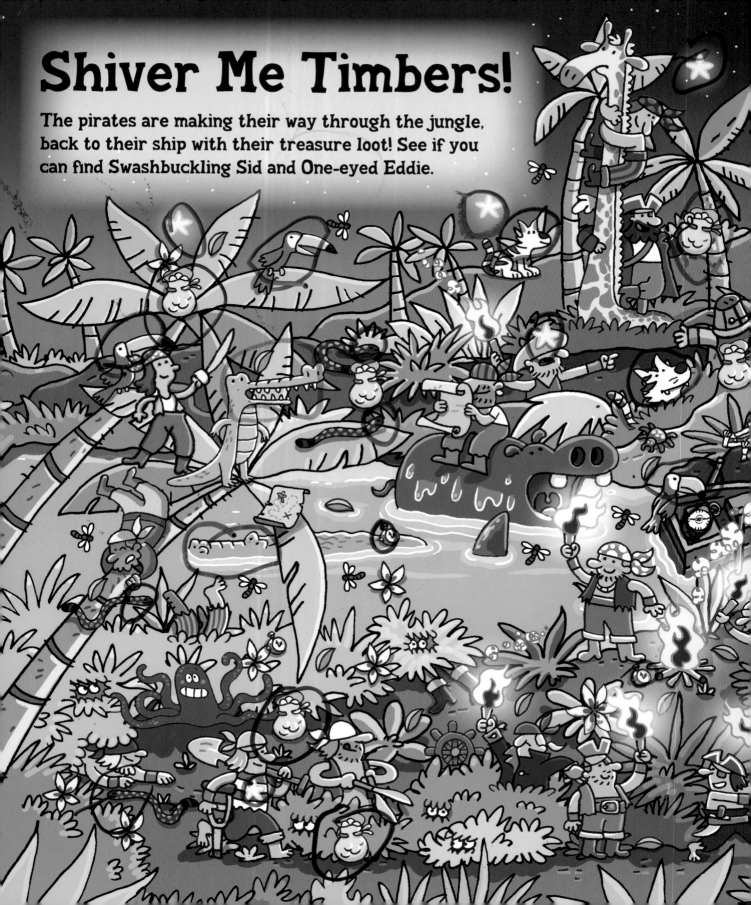

Shiver Me Timbers!

The pirates are making their way through the jungle, back to their ship with their treasure loot! See if you can find Swashbuckling Sid and One-eyed Eddie.

Can you spot these items in the jungle, too?

1 Volcano

2 Crocodiles

3 Bears

4 Tigers

5 Toucans

6 Pocket Watches

7 Snakes

8 Stars

9 Bags of Treasure

10 Tropical Flowers

20 Purple Leaves

Land Ahoy!

The pirates are visiting a nearby town to stock up on food. Can you spot Swashbuckling Sid and One-eyed Eddie? What's Swashbuckling Sid carrying?

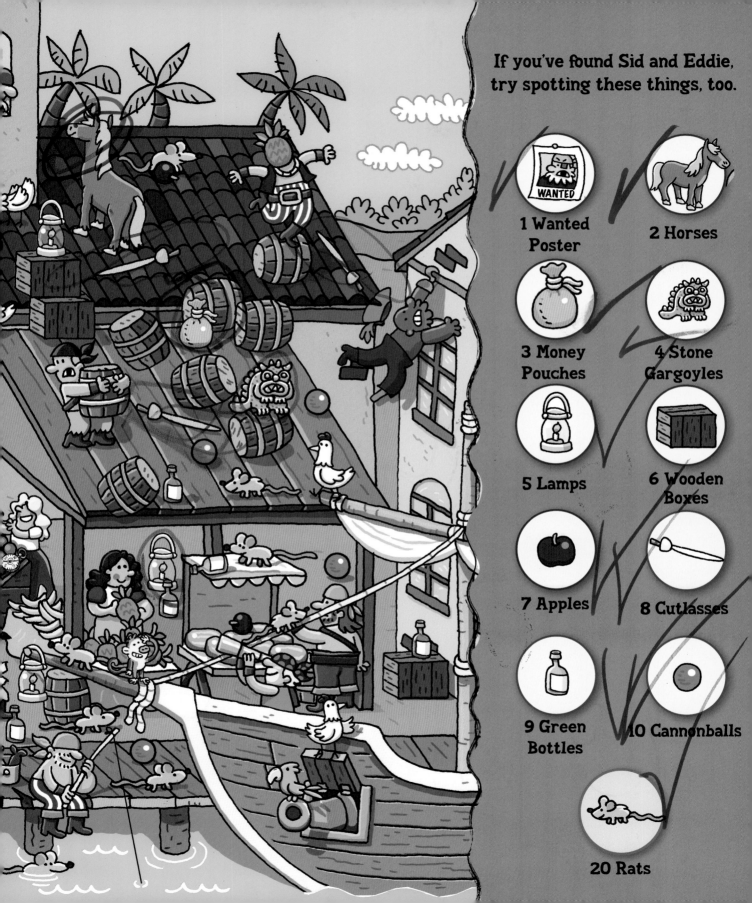

If you've found Sid and Eddie, try spotting these things, too.

1 Wanted Poster

2 Horses

3 Money Pouches

4 Stone Gargoyles

5 Lamps

6 Wooden Boxes

7 Apples

8 Cutlasses

9 Green Bottles

10 Cannonballs

20 Rats

Kitchen Chaos!

The pirates are busy preparing for a huge feast.
Can you find Swashbuckling Sid and One-eyed
Eddie amongst the chaos?

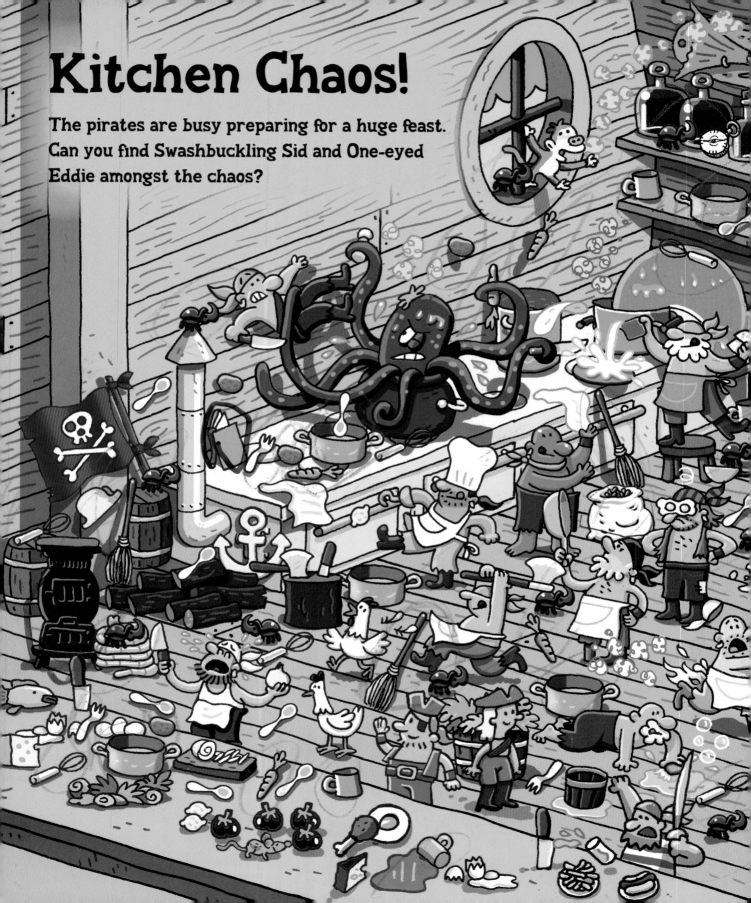

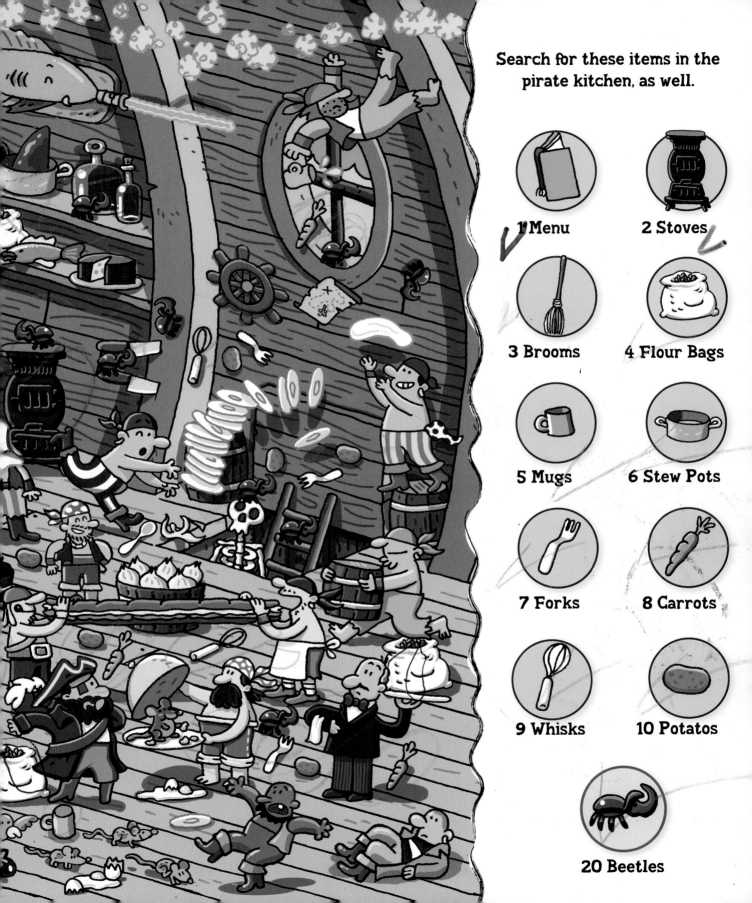

Search for these items in the
pirate kitchen, as well.

1 Menu

2 Stoves

3 Brooms

4 Flour Bags

5 Mugs

6 Stew Pots

7 Forks

8 Carrots

9 Whisks

10 Potatos

20 Beetles

A Buccaneer Banquet!

The pirates are having a banquet to celebrate finding lots of treasure! Can you spot Swashbuckling Sid and One-eyed Eddie amongst all the fun at the feast?

4 Red Spotty Bandanas

5 Mouldy Blocks of Cheese

6 Party Poppers

7 Fish Bones

When you've spotted Sid and Eddie, hunt for these items, too.

1 Accordian

2 Cakes

3 Loaves of Bread

8 Blue Balloons

9 Party Hats

10 Chicken Drumsticks

20 Boiled Sweets

Beach Scene

The pirates are relaxing at the beach today. See if you can spot Swashbuckling Sid and One-eyed Eddie having fun in the sun.

4 Picnic Hampers

5 Red buckets

6 Ice-creams

7 Yellow Towels

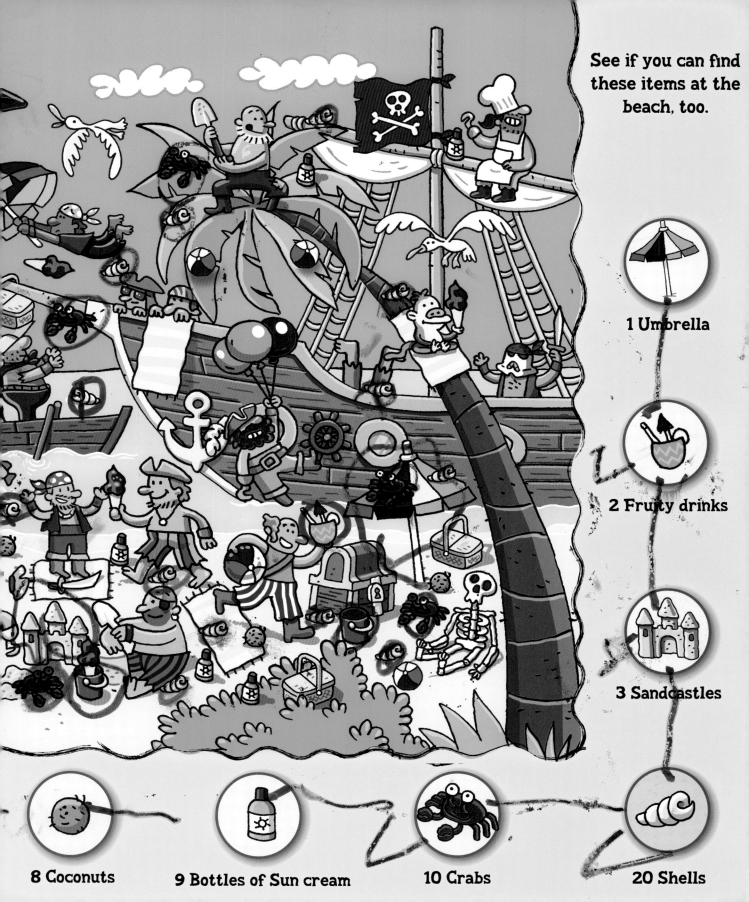

See if you can find these items at the beach, too.

1 Umbrella

2 Fruity drinks

3 Sandcastles

8 Coconuts

9 Bottles of Sun cream

10 Crabs

20 Shells

Racing

It's sports day and the pirates are having a race! Can you spot Swashbuckling Sid and One-eyed Eddie?

4 Turtles

5 Butterflies

6 Bottles of Water

7 Life Rings

Can you spot these extra pirate items, too?

1 Trophy

2 Megaphones

3 Lilos

8 Goggles

9 Cameras

10 Medals

20 Bees

Avast ye matey! You found everything on Pirate Island! Now go back and see if you can find each of these extra items in every picture, too.

1 Yellow Pirate Hat

1 Octopus

1 Monkey

1 Pirate Chef

1 Skeleton

1 Treasure Map

1 Wheel

1 Captain

1 Jolly Roger Flag

1 Anchor

1 Compass

How closely were you looking? Do you know which picture each of these items were in?

10 palm trees

10 emeralds

10 red flags

10 feathers

10 chickens

10 beach balls

10 limpets

10 candles

10 spoons

10 dragonflies